The Pool and Other Poems

by

Anthony Gardner

with illustrations by Rosanna Kelly

© 2018, Anthony Gardner
ISBN 0-936315-43-1

STARHAVEN
42 Frognal, London NW3 6AG

books@starhaven.org.uk
www.starhaven.org.uk

Typeset in Dante by John Mallinson
Printed by CPI, 38 Ballard's Lane, London N3 2BJ

Contents

Foreword

What do we look for when we read, for the first time, a poet new to us? The plural makes assumptions, of course. We are people who go in for poetry; who write it, perhaps; certainly who read it as often or as naturally as we read prose. So we are not multitudinous; we are to some degree specialists, peculiar. Nevertheless, there are more of us around than people think.

I go for music. A poem is a sonic construction in a way a letter to a bank is not. Prose is sonic also, just as much, really, in the hands of great writers. The ordering of sound is less immediate, however, it is less instantly retrievable. I have long been puzzled as to why poetry is considered a rather recondite, even highbrow form of art. It isn't. It is a quick fix. To adapt Ogden Nash, the candy of prose is dandy, but the liquor of verse is quicker. A poem has to be efficient, in the mechanical sense of the word. It employs the sounds of words and their rhythm in an arrangement which will do the emotional heavy lifting quickly. It bypasses the functional administration. You start with a "you are here" sign. The music has to set a mood immediately.

Anthony Gardner's poems are adept at creating mood efficiently. You at once become master of his state of mind. You are, in effect, writing the poem with him. He takes on universal emotions: sexual love, fear of dying, the natural world, human limitations. In his long poem about a cancer scare, The Pool, he uncovers 'a sense of love and compassion / out of time, out of fashion.' Elsewhere, he pays Blake-like attention to small moments, to the cosmic significance of the particular.

> When I opened the bathroom door,
> a spider swung down from the gloom
> into a box of washing-powder
> like the surface of the moon.

Against the galaxies, that is all the astronauts were doing.

I have long believed that poets need coaches in the way of sports people, rather than critics. 'That's your shot. That's the one to get down cold.' The only poet Anthony Gardner reminds me of a little is Coleridge, because of a shared preoccupation with mood. A more recent mood-master is Cavafy. Cavafy is also a master of place. The Gardner poems may need a change of venue. London, Cumbria and Scotland do set up preconditioned responses in a reader. I would hold onto these for inspiration but move the furniture and shift the scenery. But the mood music of Gardner's verse is compelling and addictive. You will want to read these poems many times and then demand new ones.

Grey Gowrie

For Alix
and Linda

Down the Lane

Sauntering down to the pale, surf-sluiced sands
along this narrow estuary of shade:
a rough rhapsody of rowan trees,
convolvulus and blackberries,
steeped in the scent of rain-drenched earth
on a summer's afternoon.
The voices of teenagers carry on the wind,
sharp as a shoal of rocks against the sea's rush,
carrying me back to West Cork in another century.

A girl leans back, in memory, against the harbour wall,
sun on her face, eyes closed,
jet-black hair on slim shoulders,
a dark blue jumper showing a V of skin;
and for a moment all of youth seems gathered in that corner –
its hopes, its hopelessness, its gorgeous, gawky search
for something lying out on the horizon
that we might reach if only we could master
the coiled ropes, the flapping sail,
the swinging boom, the blue-fin waves.

Tonight along the coast there's talk of meteor showers.
We make our way down to the beach
by the light of a single torch;
the teenagers swing their legs on the bridge
like shadows of our younger selves.
Out towards the point a bonfire
casts a pagan glow,
and as we watch, a harvest moon
rises from the sea,
copper-orange, gliding upwards

minute by visible minute
into a new ocean
lit by drifts of stars,
until at last it anchors
behind a reef of cloud;
and we are left to wonder whether
like that bright, transcendent sphere
the hours that we have lived and lost
might one day reappear –
as fresh as they once were,
as pristine as New Year.

Aubade

We lie here in this bed
not yet quite awake,
not yet separate shapes:
like clay in a potter's hands,
warm and inchoate.

Forgive me if I mould myself to you:
if, in this half-asleep state,
I decline to count to two,
but cling to this togetherness,
suspended like a drop of dew,
as dawn's light sketches the smoky trees
and makes the world anew.

My Uncle

My uncle never used an English phrase
if he could sing it in another language.
At Christmas in the freezing Scottish church
as bleak as skerries in a North Atlantic storm,
the rest of us bellowed 'O come all ye faithful'
as if brute British noise could keep us warm.
But his 'Adeste fideles'
was as bright as the candles' gleam
or a strong-tailed salmon launching from the water,
hurling itself upstream.

Unexpected

I drove north that December without expectations;
behind me the old year narrowed into dark lanes of disappointment.
At Penrith the night sky threw a constellation of snow against my
    windscreen;
the Whinlatter Pass was closed because of ice.
When I stepped into the brightness of a panelled hall,
you – my friend's sister – greeted me like a hero.

Three years later we married.
The windowsills of the ancient, scarcely used church
standing solitary in its field
brimmed with flowers.
And I sometimes think of those who came later that afternoon –
unlatching the door, expecting
bare stone and dampness,
and stepping instead into a dream
of scent and white blossom.

Edinburgh Revisited

'I wish,' you said, 'that we could go back
to the places we knew when we were young,
and be the age that we were then.'
But I don't wish it.
I imagine you as a student –
how you must have looked
breezing down these broad pavements,
past cobbled crescents, sooty pediments,
bluebells framed by wrought iron.
Why would you ever notice me, the older man,
standing on the corner, staring wistfully
at your unaffirmed beauty, delicate
as watercolour on ivory?

Far better, I think, to lie here now,
reaching out in the warm present to take you in my arms
as the moleskin clouds outside our window
cradle the silver moon.

Acrostic
from the French of Apollinaire

Lullaby softness, or its shadow, steals across the room.
Idly, she plays a melancholy air:
Nocturne or sentimental song, it overpowers her soul,
Deep in the shadow where her delicate fingers bring a scale to its
    close
At a piano which sighs like a woman bereft.

Seven O'Clock on a Winter's Morning

At seven o'clock on a winter's morning
the moon was a backlit bowl of curds
hanging in a still-dark sky,
hymned by over-eager birds.

When I opened the bathroom door,
a spider swung down from the gloom
into a box of washing-powder
like the surface of the moon.

And when I stepped out at eight o'clock
the whole of the London sky
was ablaze with the light of a winter dawn
like the birth of nebulae.

Closer

Could we be closer, we two?
Not unless you became me
and I became you,
and I saw me through your eyes
and you saw you through mine.
We mingle like clouds with mountain tops;
like slender shoots on a vine
stretching out in the first sun of spring
to touch and intertwine.

Hedgerow

The edges of the road
gleam with yesterday's rain;
the buttercups are drunk
on their own particular yellow.
A dandelion raises its rag-doll head;
the dock leaves climb like rusted spires
of iron basilicas.

Bicycling

Freewheeling through the woods
over pine needles and dead leaves,
the light is a stuttering symphony:
sunshine and shade, sunshine and shade;
ripples of coolness, walls of heat
in dappled alternation.
A butterfly sails with staccato grace;
a lizard darts and basks and darts,
a maestro of interruption.

Once I would have careered down this path,
racing towards the sea;
but cycling with you in your blue scarf
I prefer to take it slowly –

as slowly as can be.

At Coolure

'Come on!' you call, turning for a moment:
white limbs, a black bathing suit
silhouetted against the lake.
I hesitate, sceptical, tethered to the shore
like a somnolent motorboat:
too much trouble to rev my engine,
shed my clothes,
try the pebbled shallows.

'Come on!' you call again.
And suddenly I think, 'Why not?' and bend
to catch the moment
cast adrift on time.

The water disarms with warmth.
Up ahead, the reeds
bend like apostrophes,
and as I pass them, the sun-silvered lake
opens into tomorrow:

untrammelled,
unguessed-at,
blessed.

Nasturtiums

Like ancient phonographs in brash Art Deco orange,
the nasturtiums raise their horns to the orbiting bees.

Oh nasturtiums, play me a tune!
Play me the bees' indubitable hum;
play me the swallows' song of soar and dive;
play me the ocean's deep, hypnotic drum;
play me the crackling joy of being alive!

Requiem

for Matty, 2000-2015

I didn't think we'd get here quite so soon.
I thought there were a few more streets to go, but no:
just the question of a parking space close to the vet's door.
A journey we have made too many times before,
and now will make no more.

She made me welcome to the house at once:
before I married her mistress, became a permanent fixture,
she told me I was part of the family, beguiled me with that
    mixture
of adagio softness, beauty, joie de vivre
and such good nature as the dogless
struggle to conceive.

Try to forget her decline; remember
her glossy, rumbustious prime:
dark paw prints left in the silver dew as she raced across the lawn –
a star-chasing, floppy-eared goddess of the dawn;
her little sneezes of joy;
wild games with a wild boy;
leaps from nowhere into your lap;
crescendos of yelp and yap
excavating a dune
or badger's lair –
in tune
with all the magical scents laid bare
by that restless, questing nose.
We miss her bounding through the bracken;
we miss her in repose.

Ten days after her death, we travelled to Italy.
Our tiny hire-car grumped and harrumphed, struggling to reach
the lofty Umbrian hill towns, each
endowed with saints' lives and Annunciations
to catch the breath and cast in pale relief
our hasty cyber-age preoccupations,
reconfiguring our grasp of grief.

Unfailingly, the animals in these pictures distract us from the
        people –
even the angels with their tawny-feathered wings:
a terrier dancing to crude, pig's-bladder bagpipes;
a docile, fascinated ox upstaging the Three Kings;
and in St Francis's basilica at Assisi
those birds, those listening birds,
waiting in orderly rows to hear
heaven-sent words
too fine for human ear.

What arrogance it seems to think that we
have something that our spaniel lacked in her simplicity:
that what Church Fathers named the soul resides
only in us, and everything besides
blossoms and dies and yields up to the grave
the love that it inspired, the affection that it gave.

And so, among the pilgrims' dense, T-shirted throng,
Stranger, of your kindness, offer up a prayer
for a small black dog whose presence was a song
carried on the wakening summer's air,
whose loss our untuned hearts can hardly bear.

The Pool

i

One last length of the pool.
Typical that the sun should come out now,
just as we're about to go –
chasing the low cloud from the hills,
burnishing the slopes with heatherglow.
There's nowhere that I'd rather be than this quiet corner of
    Cumbria:
light's blessings tumble through the leaves
and flood the blue depths until they seem
celestially submarine.
Beside me pads the ghost of our old dog,
and as I turn I half expect to find her standing at the end
waiting for me to stroke her dripping ears.
Tomorrow the pool will be closed until next year,
and I wonder – when it opens again,
which of those we love will still be here?

Because it's everywhere, suddenly, the c– word:
'He's gone into hospital'; 'another round of chemo'; 'Have you
    heard?'
A friend, a friend's mother, a cousin's son –
it blazes out of nowhere like a match
and no one is safe from its deadly phosphorescence,
it's all-consuming presence,
no one.
The time we thought we had to read that book again,
sort through our holiday photographs,
skinny-dip in the rain,
make our mark in the world…

whirled away
like water down a drain.

ii

And now perhaps it's my turn.
I stare at the knot of the doctor's tie –
plump, as soft as my stomach
where the trouble seems to lie,
though nothing has as yet been diagnosed.
This is where it begins, the Blitzkrieg of mortality,
as if we've unknowingly turned a page
or broken the speed limit on life's motorway,
and all the ambulances can't keep up,
just can't keep up. Courage, people say,
is what matters in the last analysis,
and now when I need it I find there's nothing there
except the heart's appalled paralysis.
It's not a fear of nothingness, but all that comes before:
hospital sheets, the cold linoleum floor,
the visitors I love struck dumb
until – loquacious with relief – they move towards the door.

iii

Walking towards Harley Street, past buildings that have stood
for two hundred years, and may for two hundred more;
past children who could live to see
another century.
Can I forgive them? Can I find
the generosity not to mind
that they'll be here when I'm gone?
The traffic blares the warning of John Donne:

'my race/Idly, yet quickly run.'
I would go further, say that mine
seems scarcely to have begun;
I've shed my light like a streetlamp
under the rising sun.

iv

I shall be a ghost;
I shall haunt this place,
playing supernatural tricks.
I try to impress my face on the air,
mingle my atoms with the bricks.

v

Under the CT scanner, my intestines are turning blue.
I'm offered a disc of the images as a lurid souvenir.
Perhaps I'll show it at the neighbouring art fair:
'Blue Is the Colour of Fear'.

A metallic, extra-terrestrial voice
tells me to hold my breath,
and I wonder if that's how they speak in hell –
not the vague whispering of shades
half in denial of death,
but a digitised anti-humanity,
draining the viscera like a fen,
deafening us with our sinfulness.
I close my eyes, and then…

A touch.
That's what you need when you're lying there

in the throat of a state-of-the-art machine –
the hand of a fellow human, even if it's a stranger:
a bird's-wing brush of compassion
diminishing the eternal danger.

vi

Back to the specialist.
Nothing to cause alarm, and yet
the world's turned cancerous
since the two of us first met.
Mayhem in the Middle East: desperate refugees
pressed like rabbits against high fences
or flailing in hungry seas;
terrorists who renounce all vice
to glut their blood-soaked god with human sacrifice;
storms that rip trees from valley and ridge
to swell the river and crush the bridge.
What does my suffering signify?
I have lived so long in the hurricane's eye.
How can I possibly deserve
to be one of those that the fates preserve?

vii

I'm at a literary conference in Austria.
After a morning of post-colonial migration,
I escape to cobbled streets and rows of vines
surging down the hillside in waves of green and brown
until their brash fertility almost engulfs the town.

Unexpectedly, I'm beckoned by a clattering of bells.
Entering the church I see

21

the agonised *Creator Mundi*:
Christ in effigy,
bleeding from his side.
Why, in the face of such compassion,
am I not ready to die?
The profusion of cherubs and haloes,
baroque to the hilt,
weighs on me in heavy judgement.
Gold is the colour of guilt.

Later, walking by the Danube, I carve our initials in the sand:
'A loves R' they say, in adolescent play –
and there they will stay till a sea-bound barge
washes them away.

viii

The woods enact the annual sacrifice.
Copper beech and horse chestnut,
rowan and birch and oak,
they scatter the leaves from their fingertips –
such careless, spendthrift trees! –
crisp or sodden, bright or dark,
piling them to the fence-posts' knees.

By the river the raindrops fall
belatedly from their branches
catching the sunlight briefly
as we do, one and all,
shining for that moment
between sky and ground,
vanishing,
vanishing,

with barely a sound.

Oxford in deep autumn.
The mist that blurred and concealed
all along the Thames Valley
the shapes of tree and field
has given way to a blue-banner sky:
the sun's rays are angelic needles
embroidering with spires and towers
the city we once thought was ours.
More than thirty years have gone by,
and here we meet, my friend and I,
come at last to collect our degrees –
making obeisance to the Vice-Chancellor
on undependable knees
among graduates who hadn't been born
when we partied in May Day's dishwater dawn.

It's a sobering moment:
they with their lives as yet unformed,
high on possibilities;
I with those decisions taken,
dreams half-lived, convictions shaken.
And yet in an instant the disparity
is gone like the mist, and bright hilarity
binds us together, childishly merry
at the intricacy of the ceremony;
and as we pass through the great doors,
drenched with cascades of fond applause,
I wonder if heaven might be like this:
after all the suffering, disappointment, shame,

to wake to such a welcome and be told,
'The time is past for guilt and blame.
Congratulations: you've passed the test –
it wasn't easy, but you did your best;
got, in the end, more right than wrong.
Welcome to the seraphic throng.'

x

I remember my mother towards the end of her life
standing on the beach at Toberpatrick
looking out across the Irish Sea.
Did she feel the summons of infinity?
Or was it more a sense of harmony –
the wavelets scudding like a chorus line
flaunting their plumes of spray;
the foam pushing – intoxicated, brimming –
out along the strand;
the time-smoothed stones sent skimming, skimming,
from a child's hand?

xi

Good Friday afternoon at our local church.
I expect to find a handful of diehards
silently wrapped in unshared prayers –
but no, the pews are packed.
The sun falls through the stained-glass window,
giving a vermilion glow
to the black-haired woman, unimpeachably devout,
whose nationality I can never quite make out.

The service is unfamiliar, hard to follow

for one not reared within the rites of Rome;
but I stick it out, and suddenly
those hesitant voices, those disparate faces
representative of half a dozen races
blend into something unexpectedly moving:
a sense of love and compassion
out of time, out of fashion –
till I find myself one with the young and the old,
the halt and the lame, summoned to the feast.
The sun moves round the walls, and as the priest
elevates the Host, strikes my eyes
with dazzling force.
Coincidence, of course –
and yet…
And yet.

xii

Some who have come close to dying speak of floating through a
    tunnel.
That's how I feel in this subterranean pool.
It begins almost in darkness,
but as I swim, my palms push splashes of light –
magical, miniature Himalayas,
ripples of luminous blue;
and when I reach the end it opens
into a world of flowers,
leaf-rich branches,
infinite sky.

xiii

Coming in from Venice Marco Polo,

our water taxi follows the sea highway
marked out by deep-sunk pylons;
and as a seagull wheels against the cloudscape,
I wonder if that's all this life amounts to:
a boat that skims across a stretch of water
chasing the shimmering cloth-of-gold cloak trailed by the sun,
leaving – as it turns for home –
only a swallow's tail of foam.

But Venice, city of art, high altar of civilisation!
Gazing at Bellini's Madonna in Santa Maria Gloria da Frari –
the folds of her blue silk robe,
that look of otherworldly serenity
so foreign to our secular century –
I know that, failing in sainthood,
we can aspire to nothing higher, you and I,
than this:
the creation of something beautiful, transcendent,
before our time to die.
And so I write these words,
not thinking that I've done that,
but knowing that I've tried and will keep trying,
seeking that brief, elusive moment of illumination
that guides the soul home,
bright and sudden and startling as the lightning
which flashes across the shoulders of the city
on the far side of the lagoon.

xiv

I'm back in Cumbria; a year has passed.
Turning north along the fells I hear
the trickling of an unseen stream

26

beneath the buttercups and seedtime grass.
The secret life of earth!
In the far distance, a slither of Scotland splits
the blue of the sky from the blue of the Solway Firth.

Nearer, the white-painted houses catch the sun,
patches of brightness against green fields and lichened walls:
and such, I think, are the friends who give light to our lives,
leading our feet in the morning dance,
comforting us when evening falls,
awaiting us – we hope – in whatever lies beyond
when we shall all converge like fireworks sharing splendour,
spidering across the sky with legs of gold and silver,
intertwined, exultant
as we climb and spool,
gloriously reflected
in time's dark, unfathomable pool.

Like the trees that
file in silhouette
down to the
cliff's
edge .

At La Musclera

This is a moment of perfection:
the sunshine lies across the cobbles
soft in the afternoon, washing against the shadows
as the sea cajoles the headland.
In twos and threes the gulls
sally from the cliff face,
wings spread to the warm winds,
criss-crossing my view,
white defining the ocean's blue
like the arrow-wash of a speedboat
charging the horizon.
A sail gathers the breeze with trigonometric accuracy,
picking its way like a purposeful drunk
through insubordinate waves.

Today is Good Friday:
the spirit stipulates
that darkness should cover the earth,
and I wonder how to interpret such a foretaste of paradise.
Birdsong renders the speedboat's roar
a coarse anomaly,
and I guess that our business is patience:
like the trees that file in silhouette
down to the cliff's edge
gazing towards the vanishing point
of sea, cloud and haze,
waiting on eternity –
a gathering into blue.

Good Friday

The fabric of the universe torn;
a wound through which to touch
darkness and galaxies.

Snow on the Fells

Snow on the fells,
snow on the moon –
or so it appears
this still, chill afternoon.

Hoar-frost on the gate,
hoar-frost on the leaves;
rooks returning home
as thick as thieves.

If time could be frozen,
I would freeze it here:
sunlight blazing on the ice,
the world cut diamond-clear.

Metamorphosis

Lying here in my arms you feel

weightless.

It's almost as if we've dissolved, become
a warm abstraction,
a metaphor for love.
Or perhaps we're a throwback to the golden age,
when nymphs and centaurs drowsed in sacred groves,
lulled by the cicadas' dry, insistent song.

O mother Aphrodite, before dawn
drains the precious darkness from the sky,
bless this sweet fragility and trace
our supine forms across the Milky Way;
make of our embrace a constellation,
naming it for ever with our names,
that sailors lost on love's uncertain seas
may steer a course by those unchanging stars
and find a harbour deep and safe
and beckoning
as ours.

Calendar

I love you every day of the year,
including Sundays.
If I'm less attentive after midnight
and first thing on Mondays,
I owe you an apology:
the former is down to biology,
the latter to the working week.

But the week wouldn't work without you:
the days would start to creak,
and the hours and the minutes lose their lustre,
leaving me with a few sad seconds
endeavouring to cluster
back into some semblance of time,
like a barnstorming actor reduced to mime;
and the calendar nailed to the kitchen wall
would be filled with nothing –
nothing at all.

At Tretz

Provençal heat:
too hot for me, cold northern Protestant,
seeker of shade,
husbander of time,
stranger to *la dolce vita*
or its French equivalent.
But you, my love, look perfect here
with wild flowers at your feet:
a long pink skirt, a thin shirt
white and delicate as oleander.
Your happiness among old friends is like the evening light
softening the contours of Cézanne's mountain
when the sun's disc is smithied into a molten coin
and slipped into the pocket of the sky.

De Profundis

When I go back
to the dark places
of my basement life,
stumbling down the steps
to stand alone
in a dark room
remarkable only for your absence;
when I remember the wounds inflicted by others,
slow-healing,
the pain congealing
like paint in rusty tool-shed cans;
when I consider the cracked concrete,
and things thought indestructible destroyed –

Then my spirit turns to rise on the storm winds,
braving the sky paths, Hyperborean –
seeks the grace of your garden,
the salve of your smile
in sunlight,
singing.

Frogs

In the stream beside the mountain lake
the ice is beginning to thaw.
Glimpses of grass discolour the snow,
etiolated as sodden straw.

But the sun-born water seethes with life,
and as we stop to watch
resolves itself into a game
of higgled-piggledy hopscotch.

Dozens of frogs that seem to have slept
all winter long, and suddenly leapt
out of their cryogenic states,
call to their just-defrosted mates
dreamed of through the big chill,
'Do you love and want me still?'

Ah, the sweet nothings that they cloak
in that unremitting croak
sent from speckled throat and paunch,
rumbling like an avalanche
on distant slopes, to reaffirm
love's hoppy, soppy, blissful squirm!

So many princes to be kissed –
and yet you've chosen me to sing
out of them all at this sweet tryst
a soggy, froggy song of spring.

At the Ballet

Two pigeons perched on the back of a chair;
white shoulders, smooth backs, heads upon their breasts:
that's what I remember.

And then, perhaps, a transformation:

trembling into aquamarine,
Degas dancers
fluttering;
violins, an expanse of studio
swept with draperies:
carnation colours, gypsy skirts
swirling, whirling and unfurling.

That's what I remember –
and though it seems a dream,
the joy remains undimmed, unblurred
by the years in between.

Elegy: Stone Henge
for Katy Llewellyn

The ancient stones are at their greyest
in the early evening light:
lintels holding up the sky,
doorways to eternity.
I think of the scissor arch of a cathedral,
and the plain rood-screen of a country church:
all the ingenuity with which men build
buttresses against death.

ii

A city implodes with horror.
Masonry tumbles in a dry waterfall;
the skyline gapes like a broken mouth
wondering at its own obliteration:
evil scraped from the dark recesses
of a dank, corroded soul.
What can we erect in the face of annihilation?
What can the anti-matter of their hearts
fail to comprehend?

iii

My answer is here in your bedroom:
here, where we sat for the last time,
you propped against great white pillows,
your skin yellow but still beautiful,
as when I first knew you
in our young-explorer years –
a laughing girl on a bicycle,

a grail, a Matisse white bird
skimming down Lavender Hill.

This is my scissor arch,
my doorway to the blue morning:
the touch of your cheek as I leant to kiss goodbye,
and a glass of sweet peas on the windowsill
against an apricot sky –
my friend, illuminated
by all that is brave and good,
and holding it for the world
like sunlight caught in the fragile walls
of an unassuming vase.

The Populists

The concrete is cracked.
The ground is broken.
A drill like a fever rattles the teeth.
Men speak words that were better unspoken,
fracking the sump oil that lies beneath.

November

The bulb of the thermometer is a clenched fist.
The first frost sculpts the trees against a sky
mixed from purest lapis lazuli
and washed with faintest cloud;
the fallen leaves lie enshrined,
sun-touched and crystalline.

The squirrels' elegant aerobatics
sketch rhomboids over park and garden.
We stamp our feet and rub our hands
like usurers driving a hard bargain.

Acrostic for a Newborn Child

Foxgloves wait to cool her fingers;
Lilies of the valley bloom
On the path her feet will follow;
Roses scent a book-lined room
As we welcome Flora home.

Flowers of all the summer's spectrum
Educate the wondering soul –
Rainbow hints, affording half-caught
Glimpses of a perfect whole
Unseen, unknown once we are grown.
Smile and show us, new explorer,
Sunlight from the crystal hours:
Opacity retreats before you,
Nebula of all the flowers.

Open Day

Clutching maps and expectations,
the little clans ascend the campus hill.
How strangely rare it is to see
so many parents with their teenage almost-selves:
the small gradations of each physiognomy –
revised editions filling library shelves.

Waterfalls

Behind the headlong waterfalls
the pigeons hold their solemn tryst.
The cascades are their cloisters;
the pools throw out a mist
of spray as fine as incense
swung up towards a sacred vault.

Like seraphim, beyond the torrent
they wheel from shadows into light.
I gaze at them and flex my shoulders,
hungry for the power of flight.

Tudor Wedding Song

Night come swift,
With thy gift
Wrap the weary pair:
Spirits of the darkling earth
Tether every care.

Moonbeams fair
Gild the air,
Make the river bright:
Let the waves' sweet lullaby
Lap their dreams tonight.

Pain and fright
Take thy flight,
Come not near their bed;
Hide ye in the forest deep
And the mountain dread.

Sorrow's dead,
In his stead
Laughter weds the land;
Turn the glass to bride and groom
With a blessing hand.

Hourglass sand,
Thy thin strand
To the floor doth drift;
'Seize thy joys,' thou whisperest,
'For the night comes swift.'

Musings

You say you don't want to be my muse: you
feel it's like being a cardboard cut-out,
and would I please excuse you?

But I've chosen the words:
they rhyme, they scan.
The poem is written –
escape it if you can.

Afterword

'A line will take an hour maybe,' W.B. Yeats wrote of the poetic process, adding that 'there's no fine thing/ Since Adam's fall but needs much labouring.' Keats insisted that 'if poetry comes not as naturally as leaves to a tree, it had better not come at all'. The first implies that unremitting toil is at the heart of a poet's endeavours, the second that inspiration is the key. Which is right?

The answer is both. Inspiration – the image or phrase that comes unbidden – is the driving force behind any poem, and when it strikes you need to sit down and write for as long as you can, because it will never revisit you in the same way. But a good poem is rarely completed in a single session: most need to be polished and re-polished. As with any kind of writing, the first line and the last are the most challenging, and while inspiration will generally supply the first, the last can take not just an hour but several days.

For me there have been two main sources of inspiration: love and death. Many of my early poems were agonised outpourings about unrequited love; now they reflect a happier situation. Death, however, continues to encroach, and the elegies included here are ways of dealing with the other great agony, bereavement.

The Pool is based on my own intimations of mortality. It wasn't conceived as a sequence of poems, and I can't remember at what point I recognised it as such; but one poem followed another, and I found that they were linked not just by subject but by shared imagery. I found, too, that they brought together the four other principal themes that recur in my poetry and surface elsewhere in this collection: memory, art, the natural world and religious faith.

In the twilight zone between inspiration and hard labour lies poetry suggested by form, of which acrostics are an example. *Acrostic for a Newborn Child* took its cue from the great Orkney poet and novelist George Mackay Brown, whom I met through my friend (later his biographer) Maggie Fergusson. George wrote a

51

number of acrostic poems for friends' children, so when Maggie's daughter Flora was born it occurred to me to attempt one for her.

Tudor Wedding Song, with its strict rhyme scheme and archaic vocabulary, is another 'form' poem, taken from an experimental novel I wrote in my twenties using the literary conventions of a dozen different eras. I remember being asked as a student whether D.H. Lawrence was a better poet or novelist, and finding it impossible to decide – perhaps because, as Pushkin and Vikram Seth have shown in *Eugene Onegin* and *The Golden Gate* respectively, there is no clear division between the two. I suspect that every composer of haiku has at some point yearned to write an epic unrestrained by metre, and every novelist would give his or her eye teeth to be remembered for one brief, exquisite lyric. If most of my creative life has gone into novels, it is because that is what a marathon form demands, not because I set any less store by my poems; and I am deeply grateful to Chip Martin for publishing this collection, just as he did my first novel.

cover photographs by Anthony Gardner